# CHAMELEON SKY

SARAH EN KOHRS

## THE KINGDOMS IN THE WILD
## ANNUAL POETRY PRIZE SERIES

**2022**  Chameleon Sky by Sarah EN Kohrs
**2020**  Dark When it Gets Dark by Yves Olade
**2019**  All of Us are Birds & Some of Us Have Broken Wings by Ojo Taiye
**2018**  Roots Grew Wild by Erica Hoffmeister

Published by Kingdoms in the Wild Press LLC
Chameleon Sky Copyright © 2023 Sarah EN Kohrs
Cover Design: © 2023 Luna Saiteru

All Rights Reserved. No part of this publication may be reproduced, stored or transmitted in any form whether written, or electronic without prior written permission from the publisher, except in the case of brief quotations embodied in critical reviews and certain other non-commercial uses as permitted by copyright law. The views and opinions expressed herein are those of the author and do not necessarily reflect the viewpoints, policies, or position of Kingdoms in the Wild Press LLC, its owners, business partners, or employees.

ISBN-13: 978-1-7331816-3-1

## TABLE OF CONTENTS

| | |
|---|---|
| Slips of Stars | 1 |
| Under Starlight | 3 |
| By Translucence | 4 |
| Alone on a Deserted Island | 5 |
| Cherries Abloom | 6 |
| Beyond the Window | 7 |
| Fringed with Figs | 8 |
| In the Civil Twilight | 9 |
| Pseudo | Acacia | 11 |
| No Longer | 13 |
| The Other | 15 |
| The Cows of Laikipia | 16 |
| The Gilding of Peace | 17 |
| The Ambiance of Breathing | 18 |
| A Curse or a Gift | 20 |
| Bitter Stars | 21 |
| An Axion | 22 |
| Rosemary Languishes | 24 |
| Into the Becoming | 25 |
| Sheepherding on the Mountain | 26 |
| The Anatomy of a Passerine | 27 |
| The Piano Hull | 28 |
| With the Sweep of a Broom | 29 |
| After Rainfall | 30 |
| Sarah EN Kohrs In Conversation | 32 |
| Acknowledgements | |

∴ ∴

**Slips of Stars**


Like slips of stars
        that trail across the sky,
a stream cascades into pearls
        where earth ceases, for a time.

Colder than winter wind
        angled as if stove pipe
in need of remudding,
        yet ashen from overuse

as the cast iron puffs up
        a lemon-drizzled dutch baby.
The smell entices
        even children sleeping.

Even, it seems, the ones lost
        like skinks' tails, threaded
into weeping redbud roots that
        memorialize the unnursed.

I live in a place
        that breathes mist
entangled with mountain laurel,
        whose wiry wisps

uphold leafy rosettes.
        Each spring tree tulips,
orange-striped, fall into
        a run's interrupted clearness.

Twigs, petals, cones, too,
        settle or catch on rocks.
Now & then, one continues along
        the twining toward

a waterfall it does not see.
        Like a meteor. Like me.

And when I watch its trail,
        the blossom persists

downstream. Jostled,

        petals bent, filaments
awry, but still glissading across
        water that lusters with stars.

**Under Starlight**

Under starlight, between hellebores
plum-hued and butter-eyed, an eft tail
slips out, shadow becoming night.

Is the whole world petrified? Or
just my singular view, framed
by cross-hatching in a gray room

that whispers of sheerness. We cherish
so much the newborn calf, pristine;
the possibility in an uncreased

square of rice paper. If I could, what
would I fold myself into? A crane
to lift swiftly along the undulous

treeline? A lotus to weave together ravels
caught on its velveteen petals? Or, perhaps
a red eft to slip from shadow into night?

## By Translucence

If only we saw one another
by the translucence of our skin cells.

A smooth water that ripples
with the beauty of whom I see.

Polar bear strands scattered like
footprints across snow's dazzle

or a glass frog's belly with its
apparent roving of blood through

veins and whose heart beats
with the vibrancy of song.

If hyaline, would we scar less?
Scare less? Share more? Care more?

If hyaline, would we cast a vision
like the chameleon sky, whose

ethereal palette inspires every
millisecond of the day's full length?

We could wear our velveteen mantles
or place them like quilt squares

side by side. Without any awkward
pauses. And allowing room for breath.

If only I saw you / you saw me
by the translucence of our skin cells.

## Alone on a Deserted Island

| | |
|---|---|
| Plastic invades Henderson's shores | and seeks |
| acclaim as aboriginal. Like kudzu | it cloaks |
| the living—founding a new Roman | reign, so that |
| | |
| endemic species can either | acclimate or |
| bleach whiter than coral in warmed | seas. |
| They serve as tocsins amid the | toxins: |
| | |
| skeletons of the shipwrecked | stumps of |
| kerosene or resonant rosewood | harvested |
| satellite-studied atolls | untouched |
| | |
| by human presence. Pristine. | While |
| purple crabs settle into coffee pods | more foreign |
| than if the stars themselves fell | to sanctify |
| | |
| an island, adored. It's the last cairn | in a series |
| that suddenly strands refugees. | Instead of |
| enlightenment there is zugzwang. | There is |
| | |
| a lagoon, fortified to the beyond. | A great |
| wall encroached by the detritus | from the |
| Anthropocene. And there is static | silence. |

## Cherries Abloom

Silken petals unfurl from
eyed for lands shrouded in
pale red and snow
seafoam, a new ritual
quiescent buds of Sakura
of fingers folded
stripped from the gampi,
frozen mid-twirl
(like kudzu
Elephant-grey branches
poses paused
of creating something
They weep with Higans
They whisper rebirth,
They witness what
from seeing: A world
what we have come

the fairy-breath of storms
mist. When maple leaves
tints mountain peaks like
emerges from the
trees. It's as if thousands
translucent washi
into origami skirts
and draped in great nets
covering foreign soil).
coil into graceful
in the moment
almond-scented.
as ice fringes twigs.
grafted onto death.
we avert our eyes
without
to love.

**Beyond the Window**

Beyond is the light-gray world
                poised with clouds that linger
but my eyes settle not on those.
                Instead, I see a brown moth flicker
against the screen-less window
                where a trillion droplets
settle like stars. Those wings
                move in such succession, my
heart seems to speed up, too.
                I raise a hand, palm ready
for comforting, providing
                relief, hope, even.
But the window doesn't open
                and the rain drips in dirges.

**Fringed with Figs**


Fringed with figs,
        the tree's leaves umbrella bees
content to linger even when silver

rain whispers prayers
        of intercession. Each mast
hangs pendulous before it's plucked,

preventative to decay,
        they say, and 3-D print
something we'd rather might renew

like skink tails, bluer
        than lacecaps, whose roots
twine in more acidic soil.

I swat a fly. It stains
        the plastic mesh's satin weave
like the eye of a butterfly

wing. Fringed with a rising yellow,
        the fig tree glistens into a
sunrise that divides then

from now and tomorrow's
        when. Then, when I, too,
trade life's cocoon for life beyond a shroud.

**In the Civil Twilight**


clouds drape like brushed flax
as smooth as wax, honey-hued:
a gilding, more glitzy

than Mount Parnassus

while earth tries to turn away from stars.
Here, the last light hits the purpled
mountain, a still-life of pre-carded

wool dyed prematurely.

I saw it mingling within the wood.
Eyes set for chanterelles
jutting up from scallop-edged

oak leaves and Tyrian pokeweed

stalks, withering. Suddenly,
a wake of vultures pressed sky—
their primaries pointing like

fingers. Nearby, a missing calf

sprawled on the ground. Its knurled
neckbone, pallid as beeswax,
exposed to civil twilight.

This was the first time my young

son saw death so close. Not
with peaceful hands folded or
shrouded, flowered—a full-bodied scent

to cover what we don't want to be.

No, it was close enough to notice
the imbalance in the balance—
like Icarian wings melted into a form

the world remolds as civil twilight.

**Pseudo | Acacia**

Lush blossoms of a black locust
hang like velveteen testes, banded

when newborn leaves unfurl.
At 6:34 a.m. birdsong began
under the silvern quilt of a sky.

I saw it through the drawn window.
Coffee curl and bacon oven-baked

couldn't wake me as resolutely
as those toes tapping on the gutter,
sweetly known as a child. Now,

though, subsequent to thought splinters:
Am I less of a woman, with a mis-

carried womb? Less human if I
cannot regenerate like a sea star
whose vibrancy clings to blind

eyes? I want to feel normal. To look
at something that's not a reflection

of a translation. To harmonize although
my heart only echoes, jumbling.
There are no thorns to thread,

only profusions of flowers, cousins
to wisteria, mounted to a limb.

How can such a scent be so sweet
when scars settle like the moon by day?
Scars as deep as heartwood, which

cannot be castrated or cleansed.
Yes, we are a people who fear

spider silk; the scent of locust;

and, what it means to be

banded.

**No Longer**

It's like the past
was written with a white
crayon.

Slender strokes flourished
in elegant print
until

the tip dulled and
each letter began to
thicken from

a nubby stump
we continued to cling to.
We re-

moved the paper
lining. On its side, our
crayon

coated like a
cataract, a gossamer
color field

that spread. Each time
it broke, we reached
for a new

box of white crayons, the
freshness lingering on our
own

fingers, so waxy by then, we
no longer needed a
crayon.

Our loop-whorl-&
arch sheen unseen in the
writing.

And defied to recognize
the inhumanity of only
whiteness.

**The Other**

I don't have an agenda.
I'm just here.
Breathing.
.
Being.

Steeped in bleeding
leeched from crimson
sky-tides at sunrise.

I'm just here.
Breathing.
Being.

Like you?

## The Cows of Laikipia

*The cow, the goat, the sheep, the camel, mean the difference between poverty and prosperity among the pastoral communities.*
-Raila Odinga

| | |
|---|---|
| Just days before, hooves plodded | across the |
| papaya-hued hills tufted with scrub | grass |
| | |
| and bas-reliefed by wastepaper | flowers. |
| Their sedge-scent mingled with a | soft munching |
| | |
| to create the essence of | calm |
| presence. Occasionally calves butted | udders |
| | |
| whose slow drip mimicked the | trickle of rain |
| loathe to leave gravid clouds, | lacking arrows. |
| | |
| Cows roamed. Now even lions | grow leery |
| of the barbed fences, beyond | thorny acacia, |
| | |
| woven like a plaid shuka | draped across |
| a foreigner's shoulders in | welcoming. |
| | |
| But civility shivers off as Maasai | tollgate |
| roads threading the Mara, where | trespassing |
| | |
| cattle rot in the sun like bulging | buffalo— |
| to spot the plain with glistening red | beads. |

## The Gilding of Peace


A mango-colored road threads
        through the quiet bushes
spotting a grassland;
        roves along a riverbed
where salt shimmers like dew
        freshly-formed all day;
meanders forever toward
        the mountain's regal
seat on the horizon.

Of all the animals
        in that open space, the sun
finds the peace crane's
        crest to gild, as if
its slow stepping exudes
        the world's answers
to all the hardest questions.

I caress a friend's forehead,
        soft hair (the color of a third day
snow), and paper-thin skin, too
        dotted with scabbed sores.
His tongue roves uncertain of
        what to do, as the nurse
fills his feeding tube.

A salmon-colored cloth winds
        around a waist, once
strong and unpierced.
        In the end we're all
crying out for what we've
        wanted most. A friend's
warm palm pressed browward.
        Slow-steps in the sun.
And a gilding of peace.

### The Ambiance of Breathing

Wind-blown pines cling
to a precipice of silver rocks,
lichen-plated. Scrambling
toward a vortex of light
that haloes loneliness, I settle
in purview of an expanse, but
one devoid of seawaves.
Beige-prosed, charred woods
pose as lightning strikes.

No ropes. No rails. No right-
of-ways to claim. Nature yields
to anyone—a self-sacrifice often
overlooked by our constant wanting.
I could step, reach out,
and lilt off the ledge. But
without a form for flying,
I would only fall. With scaled
sight. With honey-hued

feathers dripping wet wax.
As ambient a noise as found in shells;
even settled across earth's shivery
skin. Cognizant of only self.
Do we ever stop to hear stark trees
click against other limbs nearby,
roots mingling to survive?
Do we watch the whirligig
of birds, loving one another?

Do we breathe in ridgeline
meadows, steeped with spruce?
What do our hearts halo?
Beyond the screen. Unclicked.

Hands no longer a sheen
of latex. All of us, maskless,
exposed to breathing, as delicate
to touch as moth wings, refracting
the slightest sliver of moon light.

## A Curse or a Gift

*remembering those who leave the world too soon*

| | |
|---|---|
| I saw a blue-jean sky, not | overhead, |
| but to the side. Beside & up | a red cord |
| | |
| threaded the cold crag en- | circled |
| by its own breath. From | there |
| | |
| the whole world curved | away. |
| I was beyond the zero-G | flame. |
| | |
| No birds, just breeze, | which seemed |
| to flicker the names of | those I had lost |
| | |
| like prayer flags strung | from here |
| to there. If the stars were | bells that |
| | |
| tolled for them, would we | go mad |
| without a place for silence? | The ascent |
| | |
| is like the arms of frothy | hurricanes. |
| Moments to churn. A sun | to find. |
| | |
| In that space, when there's | no more up |
| we pause in the storm's eye. | We listen |
| | |
| and listen and listen. Hoping | to hear |
| more than the beating of our | own hearts. |

## Bitter Stars

Rain raps the roof like bitter stars
through clouds that shroud the

We imagine the warmth they
measured in parallax. Ice scars

and I wonder whether clouds freeze
accustomed to suffering—scratched

so often, there's no more seeping.

how hard I press, I can never cup
as I do water / as I do something

like *what if*. I can never trace the

as I do a child's hand; fingers half
of my own. And yet, if I could, I

each breath you made and cap
firefly jars. On rainy nights when

are disregarded, I'll untwist one to
your voiceless whispers floating  like

slipping
ground.

fluctuate,
the sky

like hearts
by nails

No matter

a wall
translucent

sun

the size
would catch

them into
constellations

fill the room with
lanterns.

## An Axion

It's quiet in the kitchen.
Dawning drizzles magenta
across the pizzelle-hued

table, burnished to a waxy
gleam. Draped with
lace like a frozen lake.

There, teacups await
a tarnished welcoming,
while the kettle broods

breaching a boiling point.

Grieving is an axion.
Frizzled into starbursts.
A white rose, perfect

until it fast-forwards
into wilting, like browned
onions in a wok /

edge-etched to sienna and stems
settled in nacreous water.
I'm in that bit of quiet while

storms plasma-ball around me.

And I wonder why the sunset-
sunrise-sunset continues
its shore-broken rhythm

when all I want is for it to cease;
for everything to pause
while I learn to walk on an ice

that refuses to melt away.
Perhaps I'm scared of thawing.
Or a refreezing that keeps

me subdued from savoring

the clink of cups in the kitchen.

## Rosemary Languishes

Rosemary languishes.
    Her skeletal form hangs spideresque,
above the matte-black Jøtul,
        lit aglow when frost first tinges
autumn-dropped leaves like scraps of thread-
        painted calico on a quilt
that harvests clothes made translucent
        over time. Heat rises, seasoning
the kitchen with an aroma
        that purifies just from being.

Clippers in hand, I had walked
        among the raised beds
where crabgrass crept—always
        unexpectedly, it seems—and yet
I shouldn't have been surprised by
        the sunrise's tempering
of night's sheen and studded lights,
        as if elk might whistle again
here, in a place where they
        imploded into shadow haunts.

That moment, snipping pineapple
        sage and Siberian kale
bronze-fringed fennel and oregano;
        plucking fleshy tomatoes;
and hunting speckled eggs from
        the coop; I pause—mesmerized
by the heron's flight
        arcing overhead toward the unseen
stream, where it, too, will bide
        and glean and be
in a moment steeped with what came
        before and what will become.

## Into the Becoming

Awkward chords cling to strings     strummed
by my teen—guitar nestled on        his leg.

Poised like a snowy egret, glacial  on the coastal
plain, he says, "If I were to high- five

the sun, I wouldn't really touch it."   *No, son, you*
 *would flit into flame splayed from*   *shards*

*born of all that was before breath*    *hovered*
*and words weren't words as much*       *as dance.*

Are we really thriving in the       surviving;
strapped to something made from     something else?

The golden thread of broken         tea bowls
intimate the intricate, plucked     like chords.

Once broken and jarring, but now    as alive as
any song that time steeps into the  becoming.

### Sheepherding on the Mountain

Sunset flitters like bright prayer flags in strands
that hem the foothills. Over crags, the wind

caroms, brushes past scions, and settles
on moss matts that appear crystallized

into an iron-rich jade. Luminescent honey
gleaned a month ago or so, already drips

from the dipper. Summer's-end vines—with
their helixed tendrils—defer to a displaced season

as snow fills the montane when harvesting
knives poise above grape clusters. Ice

petroglyphs the edge of the river, where
fish flap and bends wend into horseshoes.

Bighorn sheep roam the Sierra—their bells
tinkling in time with hooves that clink

across the rocky terrain. Devoid of man's
fingerprints, the sky fills with flaming jewels,

lighter only than the moon, which simpers,
fades, and reappears in predictable patterns.

More predictable than the wind, than the snow's
first falling beyond the mountain's peak

than the quavering of human hearts
poised in a displaced season.

## The Anatomy of a Passerine

Pneumatized bone enables flight, as
        native to living as breath.

Tressed within, woven, fibrous.
        Could they flute a tune as sweetly

as when voice welcomes dawn?
        A springlike furcula

mimics antennae musing on
        more than the heart's lilt.

It settles on the sternum
        like a heraldic unknot,

claiming what we would wish:
        fused phalanges striking the sky

as deftly as oars dipping into water. I
        imagine the loss of writing,

of molding clay on a turning wheel,
        of holding the hand of someone I loved,

should I have wings instead. Could I
        withdraw from such touching? Even with

skin akin to silk; even with wind-dancing;
        even with a ready song of hope.

Could I, native to being in a world
        formed by many breaths, withdraw;

tressed within by musings
        of what humanity can only wish?

## The Piano Hull

bleeds unfurling sheets of smoke.
The piano, whose hull spirals fiery

flecks counterclockwise into sky.
Its crackling echoes cows munching hay

while night ceils everything.
Fingerlike flames slip along slats

devoid of even melancholy melody.
And still the moon won't shine.

How many times did tree buds
rupture into fringe before the wood

proved ready for gleaning, planing
smooth, wiring for sound?

And now the piano kindles,
warming a crowd one last time

without the wince of chipped keys
that extend into skeletons rattled, silently,

behind boxed forms devoid of doors
where music once required a tracker bar.

Clouds fray into saltless rains they
release to saponify what remains,

while the hull slips a smoky cadence
whose spiral openly aims starward

in a silent passage I will one day
know, and so, too, us all.

## With the Sweep of a Broom

Bristles whisk away soil
unlaced near the swing,

when winds blow] & seeds
tufts of spooled candy,

twirling outstretched arms
& shells [often crushed

into orange clay yearning
glint] & sand [that landed

beach towels, dripping-dry
& skins [shed to form a

translucence that only time
from its morning mist] &

whose grit forms pearls
expected—all swept away

threnodies swell from
as everything settles under

[conveyed by shoes
creaking

[puffed up like
some / others

all the way down]
ready-to-knead

for an opaline
from flapped

along a rail]
ghastly

can dissipate
scraps

we never
while

flagellating chimes
worn floorboards.

## After Rainfall

With the subtle rise of morning, I notice
the unmuntined glass, littered with rain-
drops and stretched as taut as wet shore

where shells settle like cairns, collapsed.

Each cold stone is a hardened heart. Heaped
for centuries. Expansive as wasteland. Some,
freshly set. Yet, they all remember the scarring.

A child would only see a source for skipping

the weight of things across water's skin
or clouds blushing when lightning illuminates
even the reflections of a silent puddle.

I wait for shadows to snare the wind, too

whose cold fingers broke the limb of a redbud
drooped in mourning over my child's grave.
But nature knows no laws of compassion.

Only the rise and fall of how now becomes
then becomes now.

# SARAH EN KOHRS

IN CONVERSATION

**How did *Chameleon Sky* come to be?**

*Chameleon Sky* began as a study of blue, which symbolizes everything from introspective journeys, like the blessingway of an Ancestral Puebloan or the peregrinatio of the ancient celtic pilgrim, to wisdom to depression. The sky is pervasively blue. And yet, not always. In ruminating over my own life journey, I recognized that everything belonging to the sky creates a palette that every single person can appreciate from where they are on Earth. Sometimes the ethereal hues are extravagant; other times seemingly dulled as if viewed from underwater. Like a chameleon, which has a 360° arc of sight around its body, the sky cradles our oblate spheroid, our Earth, us. It's comforting to consider how the sky is an inspiration and a comfort to each of us across the globe.

**Were you trying to tackle a particular subject, theme, or topic and why? How have these changed over the years?**

When I had my second miscarriage, I recognized the pain of that moment would become a pearled memory over time. Most of the poems in this chapbook come from my time as a homeschooling mother of young children. The sacred embrace of the sky is similar to the traditional view of a mother figure in a family setting. The sky's rhythm continues even when we experience moments that seem to stop our hearts: guttural loss or overflowing joy. *Chameleon Sky* seems to shimmer with the question: does the sky become what we need or do we define ourselves by what the sky needs us to see? How will that answer differ from me to you? From place to place?

**You have a background in Classical Languages and Archeology, how has that shaped your writing? Do you find yourself trying to explore those fields through your poetry?**

My writing is most definitely impacted by classical languages and archaeology. I love the literary devices I learned in translating ancient authors, such as Ovid, Horace, and Homer. For me, it is meaningful to reimagine the golden line or how metonymy and enjambment can add depth of meaning to modern poetry. I view my work as a wordsmith and use the topics that draw my own attention to create compelling imagery that resonates a relational understanding.

**What does your writing process look like?**

Sometimes, my writing process feels like Penelope unweaving Laertes' burial shroud each night while Odysseus is voyaging. What I write one day may change completely another day. Regardless, my process always involves research. I draw on mythologies and stories I have read, as well as encyclopedia entries on less familiar topics, like guanine nanocrystals (the structures in skin layers of a chameleon that reflect light differently depending on how they are stretched or relaxed) or biogenical fluorescence (the ability for certain species of chameleons to emit a bright blue glow from their bones).

I keep paper scraps or small notebooks, along with pens, everywhere I might find myself: in the car, in my bags, by my bed, in my pottery studio. I also have a journal for words that I love. In addition to the word's meaning, I'll write the etymology of the word - especially if it's ancient Greek or Latin.

It's amazing how researching the source of words can cast more depth for its use in a poem. Often images tie together, so that once I jot down one, another emerges seamlessly. Then, my poems come out similar to how Dillard describes her own writing in *The Writing Life*: "these things fill from behind, from beneath, like well water" (1989:78). I keep a poetry template on my desktop, so that when a poem begins its emergence following an inspiration or research, I can work through it for as long as I can - returning to it as I am able. Then, I let it rest for a little while and revisit it when my reading of the poem feels fresh. Sometimes that is the next day; other times, I still am not ready after a year.

**Covid-19 has had such a huge impact on our world over the last 2+ years, how has it changed how you view and/or navigate and experience the world?**

The pandemic has made me more aware of how I focus my time. I have trimmed off several roles that I loved, but were no longer best for me. They took away from the creative arts that I love so much. While the creative arts in my life (especially as a homeschooling mother with three children) still align with an image of water poured into a container of rocks, I have removed some of the rocks so that more of the arts can fill my life. I want these creations to impact others in a positive way, as much as they bless my own life.

**Where do you see yourself and/or your work this time next year? Any big goals, or projects on your mind?**

As it did to so many communities in the United States, the pandemic brought a rolling boil to racial justice issues in Shenandoah County, Virginia, where public schools were renamed from Confederate generals to geographically-significant aspects of the natural landscape. This change for a more positive and inclusive identity was an act of compassion by our school board.

However, as always happens with change, many in our community were not happy with the school name change. I have been working on a poetry and photography project that captures *An American Profile* here in this place against the backdrop of our county's history, steeped in practiced slavery and injustice toward minorities, and encourages a better way forward when that perspective is steeped in empathy. This poetry book reimagines where we place our pride and how we walk with our neighbors in grace.

**What other art form influences or informs your writing?**

I practice pottery and photography, in addition to writing. Often, when I have been working in my pottery studio, poetry naturally emerges. The digital images I capture via camera often lead to poems, similar to ekphrasis. For example, the concept for my next poetry book came from an image I captured from a broken wall in an abandoned building.

The photograph, *American Profile*, was published in *Reservoir Road Literary Review*'s Issue 5 in 2021. There are times when I use documentaries, like encyclopedia entries, to help guide my research for writing. Or if there is a song or artwork that connects to the topic at hand, I'll use that as a source of inspiration, too. One example of this is a poem, "When all the World," that I wrote about cave paintings in Argentina, *Hands at Cuevas de las Manos*, and which won the 2021 Ekphrastic Poetry Award for Poetry Society of Virginia.

**What has been the hardest part of this year regarding your creative work?**

In July, our family traveled to the Pacific Ocean and back home again. The next to last night of our journey, someone smashed our van's passenger-side window and stole five bags, three of which were mine. One of these included my laptop, nestled in the very back of the van under our Maasai shukas. We had gotten into our hotel very late and were leaving very early–it was the only time on the journey that I had left my laptop in the van. The loss of that tool and the roughly three months of writing that I had not had time to backup was immense. And yet it reminds me of the ephemeralness of our own lives, as well as the lack of guarantee we have in living.

**What has been the most rewarding part of the last 12 months?**

One of my writing goals has been to have a published poetry book. Having *Chameleon Sky* chosen by Kingdoms in the Wild for its 2022 poetry award has definitely been the most rewarding part of the last 12 months. I'm grateful for the opportunity to share my writing in this way, as well as the contemplative conversation this chapbook orchestrates with its readers.

**What's an underrated (or little recognized) book you love?**

I love a variety of books. As a homeschooling mother, one of my favorite books to read to my children was *The Lion and the Little Red Bird* by Elisa Kleven. It's a story about a bird that loves to paint and a bird that is enchanted by the lion's tail, which changes color each night. They do not speak the same languages, but by sharing their life journeys with one another, they discover they do not need to. Each one can relate to the other and appreciate the beauty that emerges from their respective journeys.

Marc-Alain Ouaknin's *Mysteries of the Alphabet* is another underrated book. This book holds a quote by Jabès, which summarizes its explorations of the alphabet well: "Words are grouped around a picture like men [and women] around a table or a log fire..." (1999:127). I love the imagery of language this evokes, also resonant in the children's book I mentioned. I enjoyed reading Beatrice Hohenegger's *Liquid*

*Jade: The Story of Tea from East to West*, as much as *Sweet Like Jasmine: Finding Identity in a Culture of Loneliness* by Bonnie Gray.

I would be remiss if I didn't also mention Desmond Tutu's *No Future Without Forgiveness*. Tutu writes of the cathartic effect of telling our stories. I think if all of us are more willing to hear one another's stories - especially those whom suffering has touched so poignantly - many of our world problems would be solved and our responses to one another would sparkle with much needed compassion.

**What's your favorite way to unplug: book: movie?**

I live only eleven miles from the George Washington National Forest, which is a wilderness area in the Appalachian Mountains that was designated in 1918, largely to re-establish tree growth from mountains that had been logged so heavily that eroded soil was clogging the Chesapeake Bay watershed. I love taking my sons hiking on trails that crisscross this wilderness. Now and then, we will pack hammocks, art and writing supplies, nature identification books, and enjoy the stony creeks or remote overlooks. Walkabouts or forest bathing are as meaningful for me as throwing clay on a potter's wheel.

**Where can readers find you?**

My website is senkohrs.com. There readers can explore links for Visual Art and Writing publications, discover the festivals and readings in which I will be participating for the coming year, and learn more about one of my writing projects, a blog entitled "52 Weeks." In addition, find me on Instagram at SARAHENKOHRS or Facebook at SENKCREATIVEARTS.

## ACKNOWLEDGEMENTS

"Beyond the Window" in *Bluebird Word*, 2022.
"An Axion" in *Wild Roof Journal,* Issue 15, 2022.
"A Curse or a Gift" in *Stoneboat Literary Journal*, Issue 12.1, 2022.

## ABOUT THE AUTHOR

Sarah E N Kohrs is an artist and writer with over 90 publications in literary journals, including poetry in *Crosswinds Poetry Journal, Cumberland River, Elevation Review, From the Depths, Poetry from the Valley of Virginia, Rattle, Watershed Review, West Trade Review, the winnow;* photography in *Blueline Literary Magazine, CALYX, Columbia College Literary Review, Esthetic Apostle, Glassworks, In Layman's Terms, Mt Hope, Ponder Review;* and both in *Claudius Speaks, Raven Chronicles,* and *Virginia Literary Journal.* Her "Along the James" won Virginia Conservation Network's Our Common Agenda 2021 photo contest; and, "When All the World" was the 2021 recipient of Poetry Society of Virginia's Ekphrastic Poetry Award. Sarah has a BA in Classical Languages and Archaeology from College of Wooster, Ohio, and a Virginia teaching license endorsed in Latin and Visual Arts. Life experiences that bolster her art include homeschooling, creating pottery for local Empty Bowl suppers, volunteering as an Extension Office master gardener, and serving as a board member of Valley Educational Center for the Creative Arts (VECCA). Where to find Sarah EN Kohrs: SENKOHRS.COM

**KINGDOMS IN THE WILD PRESS**

Is a home for poetry and fiction and in-depth conversations about creativity by emerging and established authors. We strive to bring you work that reflects the world's complex and intertwined cultures and histories. Read more work on our website: KINGDOMSINTHEWILD.COM

Made in the USA
Columbia, SC
18 February 2023